MEL BAY'S
JAZZ GUITAR PHOTO CHORDS
BY COREY CHRISTIANSEN

2 3 4 5 6 7 8 9 0

© 2006 BY MEL BAY PUBLICATIONS, INC., PACIFIC, MO 63069.

Visit us on the Web at www.melbay.com — E-mail us at email@melbay.com

Table of Contents

Introduction

Jazz Guitar Photo Chords presents the most common jazz guitar chord voicings and shapes via standard notation, tab, chord diagram, and a photo of what the chord looks like when played on the guitar. This will be a great jump-start for aspiring jazz guitarists who need a lot of chord voicings and shapes fast. This method of learning is perfect for school jazz band guitarists or anyone else who is just starting to cut their teeth playing jazz.

These chords are moveable shapes. This means that by knowing the names of the notes on the fretboard, the shapes presented can be played in virtually every key. The concept of moveable chords is invaluable for all guitarists. It allows us to learn a single shape, and by moving that shape around the fretboard, the chord can be played in every key. All you need to know is where the root (the note that names the chord) is. Page 6 has charts that will help you understand the layout of the fretboard. We're not going to show you every chord in every possible key in this book, but if you understand the concept of the moveable chord, you can fill in the missing pieces. Be sure to learn each shape not only in the single key presented, but in all twelve keys. You will not only learn 12 times more chords, but learn the layout of the fretboard. There will be some information on how this is done throughout the book.

There are many choices for each chord found in this book. It is up to the player to decide which one would sound the best in any given circumstance. Be sure to experiment with many of the voicings that are found in this text and begin combining them with others over common jazz standards. A vocabulary of personal favorite chord sounds and chord movement will soon follow. Also, be sure to always keep track of where the root note (the note that names the chord) is located within the shape of the chord. It isn't always on the lowest sounding string of the voicings.

How to Use This Book

Below are explanations for the fretboard diagrams and tab that are used in the book. Standard notation and photos are also used to help students learn what notes are used in each chord and to help them see what the chord literally looks like when played on the guitar.

With the chord diagrams, the vertical lines represent the strings on the guitar, with the first string being on the right. The horizontal lines represent frets, with the first fret being on the top. Dots, or numbers, on the lines show the placement of left-hand fingers. The numbers on, or next to the dots indicate which left-hand finger to use. A diamond may be used to indicate the placement of the root of the chord or scale. Root refers to a note which has the same letter name as the chord or scale.

A zero above a string indicates the string is to be played open (no left-hand fingers are pushing on the string). An "X" above a string indicates that string is not to be played, or that the string is to be muted by tilting one of the left-hand fingers and touching the string lightly.

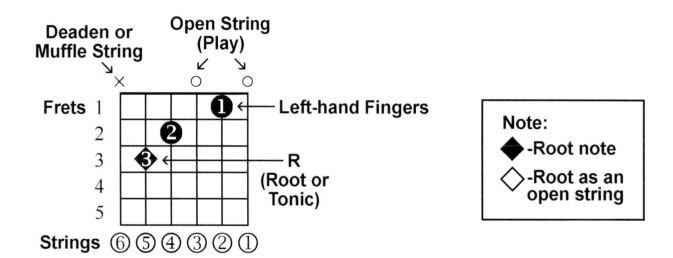

Tablature

One way of writing guitar music is called tablature. The six horizontal lines represent the strings on a guitar. The top line is the first string. The other strings are represented by the lines in descending order as shown below.

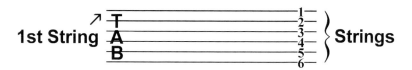

A number on a line indicates in which fret to place a left-hand finger.

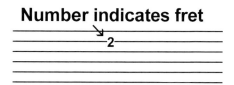

In the example below, the finger would be placed on the first string in the third fret.

1st String, 3rd Fret

If two or more numbers are written on top of one another, play the strings at the same time.

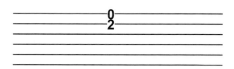

Root Notes and Moveable Chord Shapes

Many of the chords presented in this book are moveable. This means that the shapes can be moved into different frets to create a different chord name. For example a G7 chord moved up two frets becomes an A7 chord. All one has to know is where the root (the note that names the chord) is located within the shape and where all of the notes are on the fingerboard. The following charts show where all of the natural notes are on the guitar fingerboard. The sixth and first string have the same fret and note name relationship; they are just two octaves apart. Remember to sharp (♯) a note, raise it one fret. This means to move it one fret closer to the body of the guitar. To flat (♭) a note, lower it one fret. This would be to move it one fret closer to the head of the guitar. Ok, now every chord presented can be played in all 12 keys. Notice that the root note is not always played in the lowest position. When a note other than the root is played in the lowest position it is called an inversion and is written as a slash chord. For example, G7/B. This means a G7 chord with B in the bass. Inversions sound great and have many uses so don't let the slashes bother you when learning these chords, the slash is only communicating which note is in the bass.

Root Notes On The Sixth and First String

0	1	3	5	7	8	10	12
E	F	G	A	B	C	D	E

Root Notes On The Fifth String

0	2	3	5	7	8	10	12
A	B	C	D	E	F	G	A

Root Notes On The Fourth String

0	2	3	5	7	9	10	12
D	E	F	G	A	B	C	D

Root Notes On The Third String

0	2	4	5	7	9	10	12
G	A	B	C	D	E	F	G

Root Notes On Second String

0	1	3	5	6	8	10	12
B	C	D	E	F	G	A	B

The following chords are voiced on strings 6, 4, 3, and 2. For each four-note chord, the root position is shown as well as all of the inversions. Some of these may not sound good alone but be sure to practice playing them in chord progressions over jazz standards. Many of them work great as passing chords. Sometimes, when learning by chord shapes, trial and error is the best teacher.

Most of the chords in this book are presented in the key of G. For chords with the lowest note on the 6th string this allows the player to see all of the inversions in an orderly fashion as they work up the neck.

Sixth String in the Bass Chords
Maj7 Chords

G Maj7

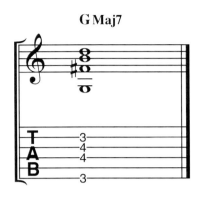

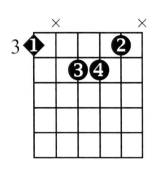

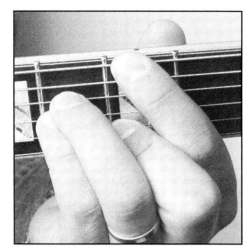

G Maj7/B

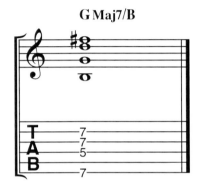

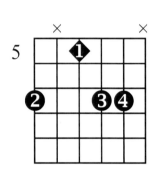

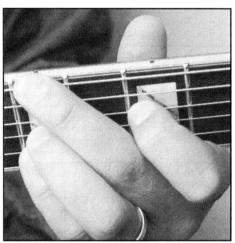

G Maj7/D

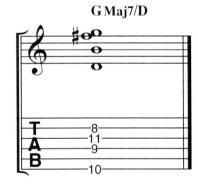

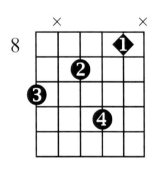

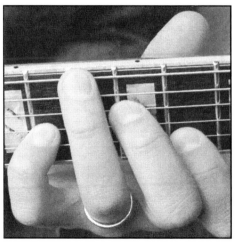

G Maj7/F♯

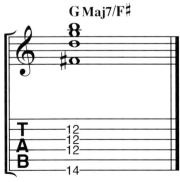

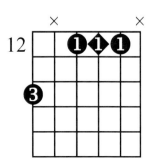

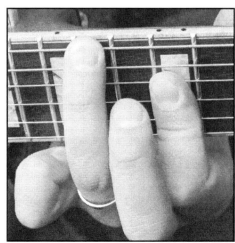

Note: the chords on this page are moveable and can be played in any of the twelve keys. See page 6 for more information.

7th Chords

G 7

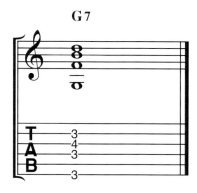

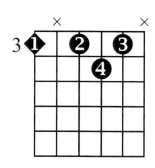

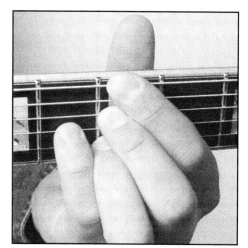

G 7/B

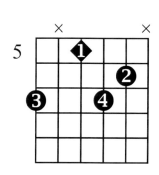

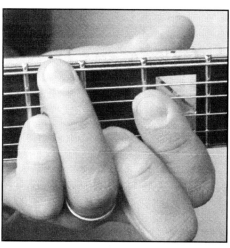

G 7/D

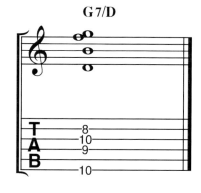

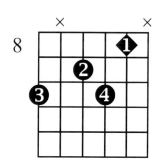

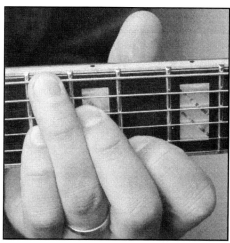

G 7/F

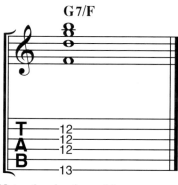

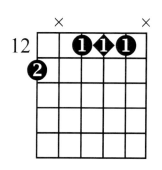

Note: the chords on this page are moveable and can be played in any of the twelve keys. See page 6 for more information.

6th Chords

G 6

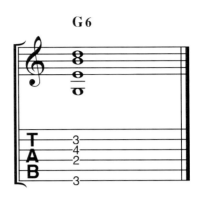
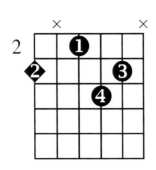
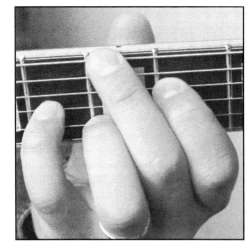

G 6/B

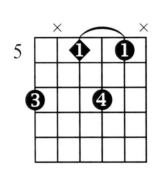
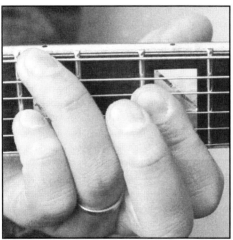

G 6/D

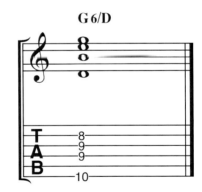
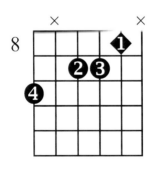
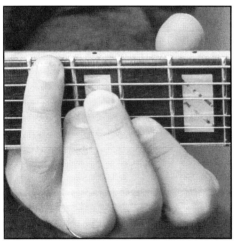

G 6/E

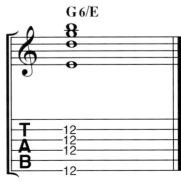
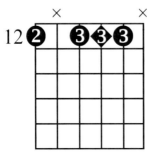
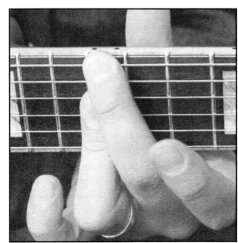

Note: the chords on this page are moveable and can be played
in any of the twelve keys. See page 6 for more information.

m7 Chords

G m7

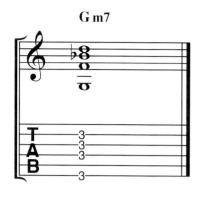

3

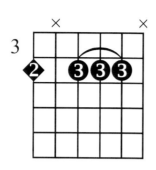

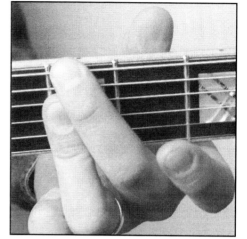

G m7/B♭

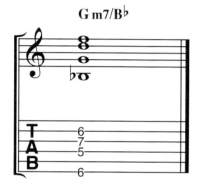

5

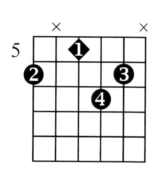

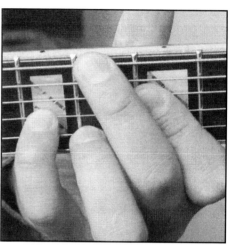

G m7/D

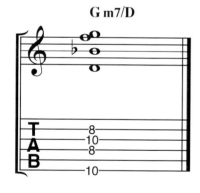

8

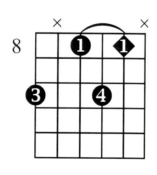

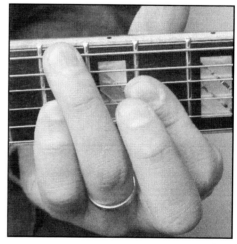

G m7/F

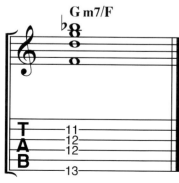

11

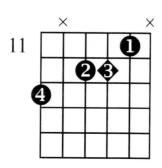

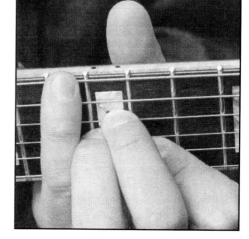

Note: the chords on this page are moveable and can be played in any of the twelve keys. See page 6 for more information.

m6 Chords

G m6

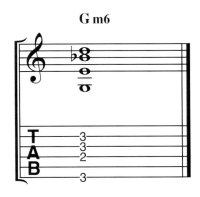
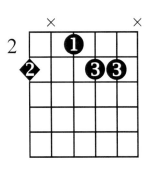
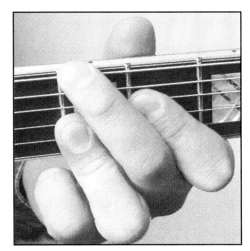

G m6/B♭

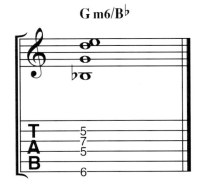
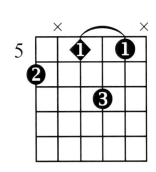

G m6/D

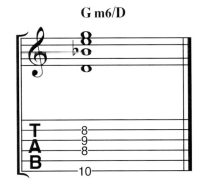
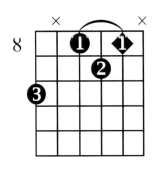

G m6/E♭

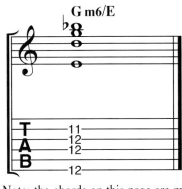
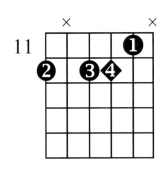
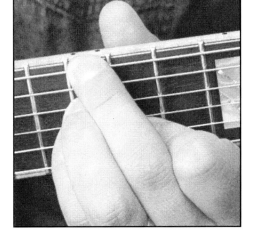

Note: the chords on this page are moveable and can be played in any of the twelve keys. See page 6 for more information.

m7(♭5) Chords

(°7)

G m7(♭5)

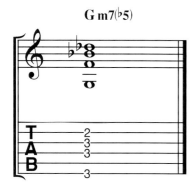

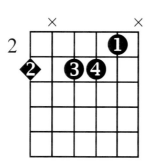

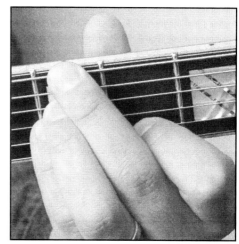

G m7(♭5)/B♭

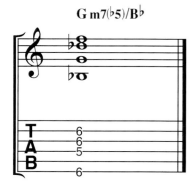

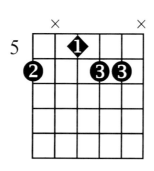

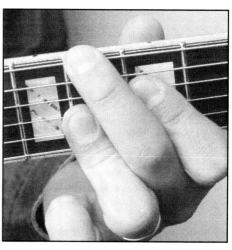

G m7(♭5)/D♭

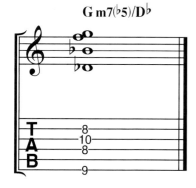

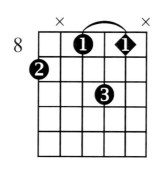

G m7(♭5)/F

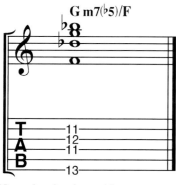

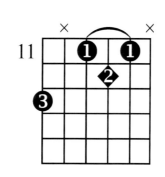

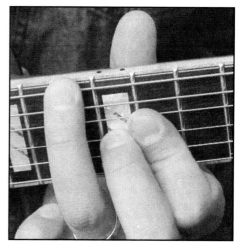

Note: the chords on this page are moveable and can be played in any of the twelve keys. See page 6 for more information.

Diminished 7th Chords

(dim7 or °7)

G dim7

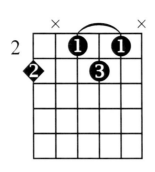

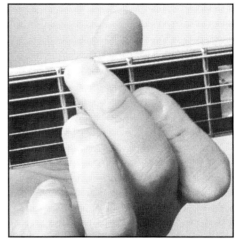

G dim7/B♭

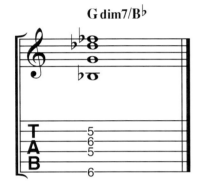

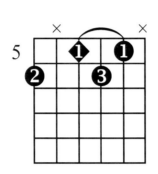

G dim7/D♭

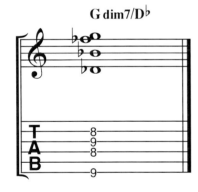

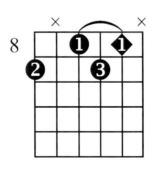

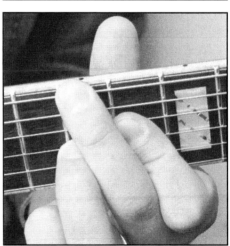

A diminished chord has a ♭♭7 interval. F♭, C♭ and many double flat notes often are written with their enharmonic name. F♭ and E are actually the same pitch. These chords have been written this way to show both possibilities of notating the correct bass note.

G dim7/E (F♭)

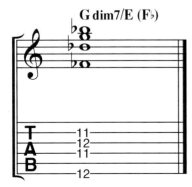

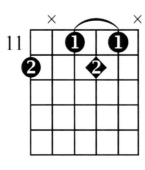

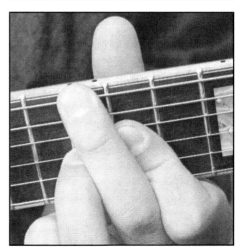

Note: the chords on this page are moveable and can be played in any of the twelve keys. See page 6 for more information.

The following chords make use of strings 5, 4, 3, and 2.

Strings 5, 4, 3, 2

Maj7 Chords

C Maj7

TAB
```
5
4
5
3
```

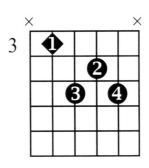

3

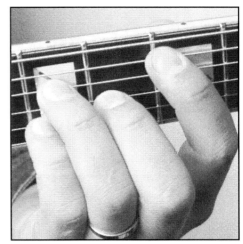

C Maj7/E

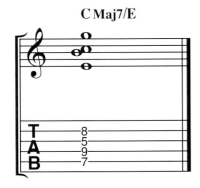

TAB
```
8
5
9
7
```

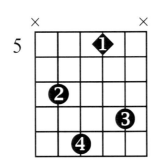

5

C Maj7/G

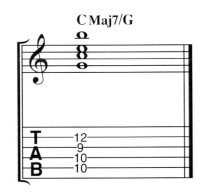

TAB
```
12
9
10
10
```

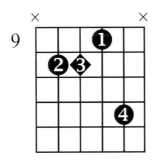

9

C Maj7/B

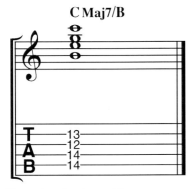

TAB
```
13
12
14
14
```

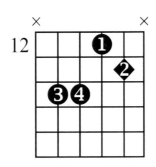

12

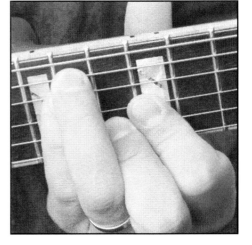

Note: the chords on this page are moveable and can be played in any of the twelve keys. See page 6 for more information.

7th Chords

C 7

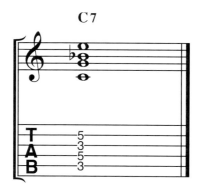

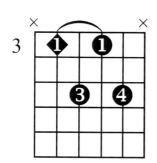

C 7/E

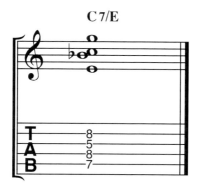

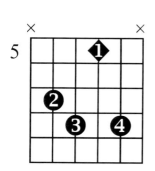

C 7/G

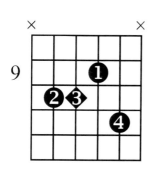

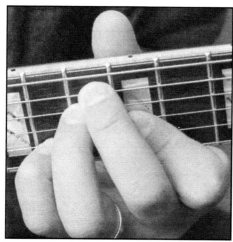

C 7/B♭

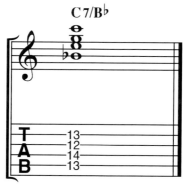

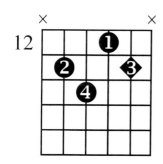

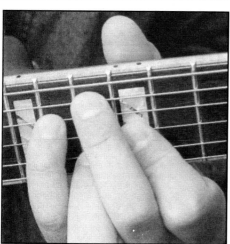

Note: the chords on this page are moveable and can be played
in any of the twelve keys. See page 6 for more information.

6th Chords

C 6

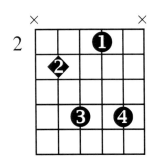

C 6/E

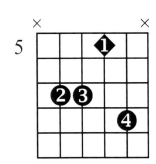

C 6/G

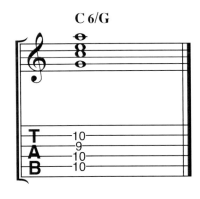

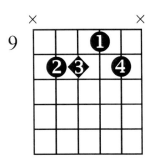

C 6/A

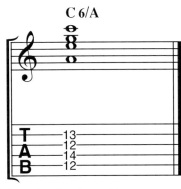

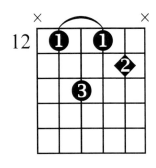

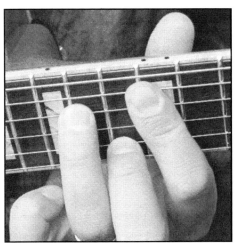

Note: the chords on this page are moveable and can be played in any of the twelve keys. See page 6 for more information.

m7 Chords

C m7

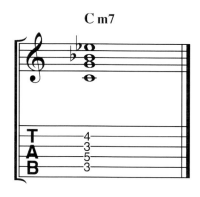

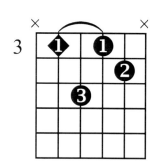

3

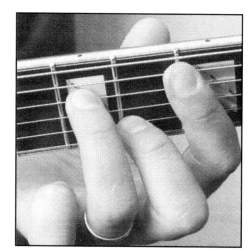

C m7/E♭

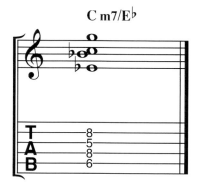

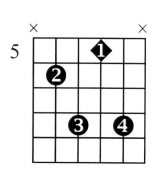

5

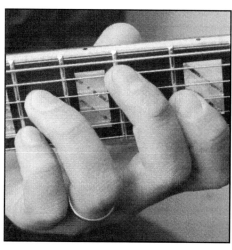

C m7/G

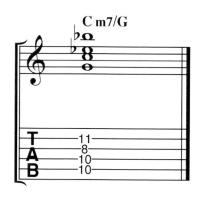

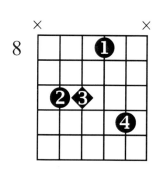

8

C m7/B♭

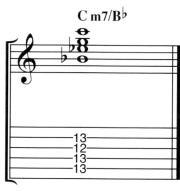

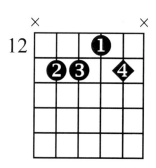

12

Note: the chords on this page are moveable and can be played
in any of the twelve keys. See page 6 for more information.

m6 Chords

C m6

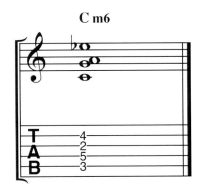

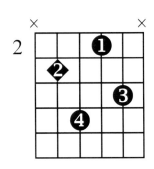

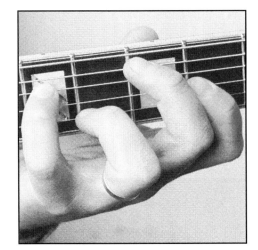

C m6/E♭

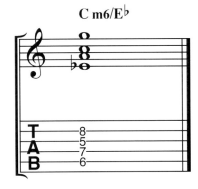

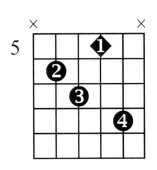

C m6/G

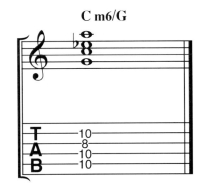

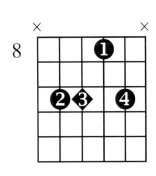

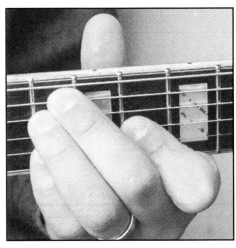

C m6/A

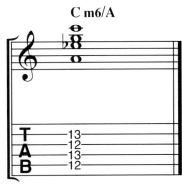

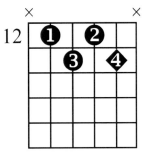

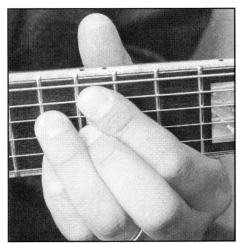

Note: the chords on this page are moveable and can be played in any of the twelve keys. See page 6 for more information.

m7(♭5)

(°7)

C m7(♭5)

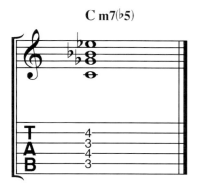

3

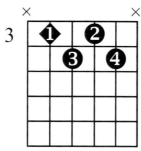

C m7(♭5)/E♭

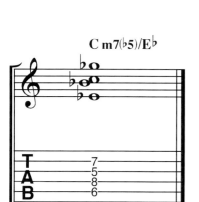

5

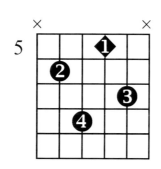

C m7(♭5)/G♭

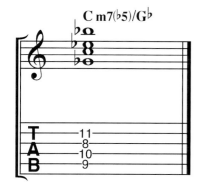

8

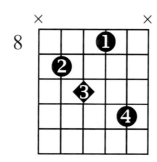

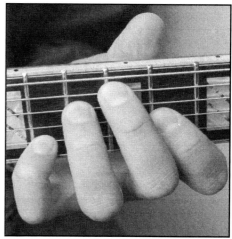

C m7(♭5)/B♭

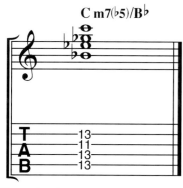

11

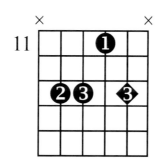

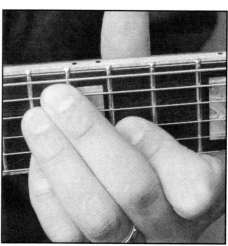

Note: the chords on this page are moveable and can be played
in any of the twelve keys. See page 6 for more information.

Diminished 7th Chords

(dim7 or °7)

C dim7

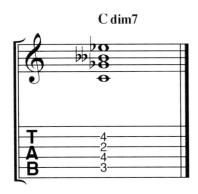

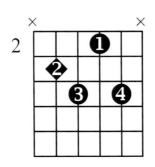

2

C dim7/E♭

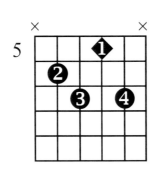

5

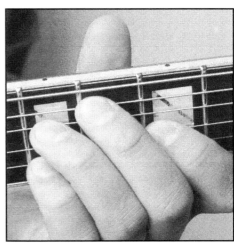

C dim7/G♭

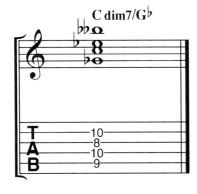

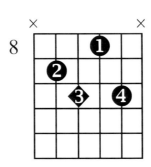

8

A diminished chord has a ♭♭7 interval. Double flat notes often are written with their enharmonic name. B♭♭ and A are actually the same pitch. These chords have been written this way to show both possibilities of notating the correct bass note.

C dim7/A (B♭♭)

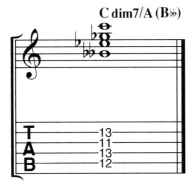

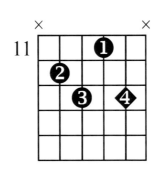

11

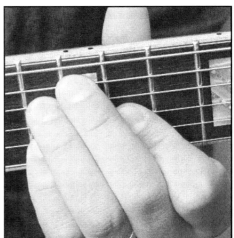

Note: the chords on this page are moveable and can be played in any of the twelve keys. See page 6 for more information.

These voicings are closely related to the shapes found on strings 5, 4, 3, and 2. The order of the notes in the voicings are pretty much the same, but they use strings 4, 3, 2, and 1. These are wonderful shapes to use when using sparse or light comping behind soloists or in small group settings.

Maj7 Chords

G Maj7/F#

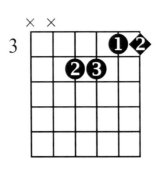

3

G Maj7

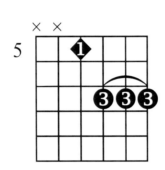

5

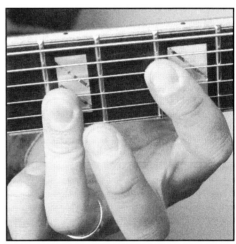

G Maj7/B

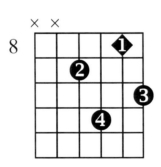

8

G Maj7/D

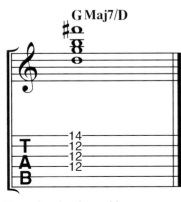

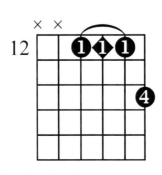

12

Note: the chords on this page are moveable and can be played in any of the twelve keys. See page 6 for more information.

7th Chords

G 7/F

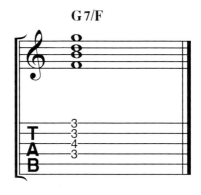

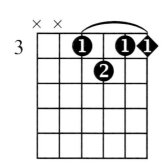

3

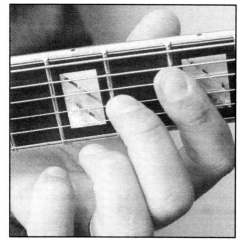

G 7

5

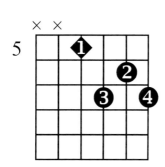

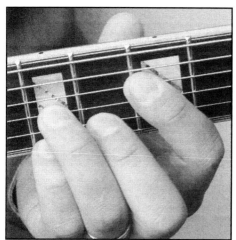

G 7/B

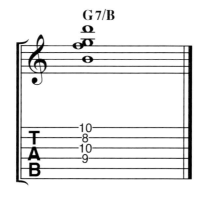

8

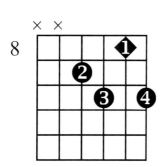

G 7/D

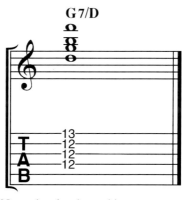

12

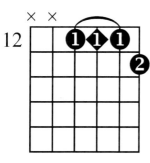

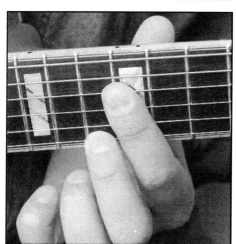

Note: the chords on this page are moveable and can be played
in any of the twelve keys. See page 6 for more information.

6th Chords

G 6/E

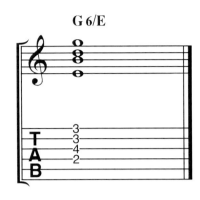

```
T  3
A  3
B  4
   2
```

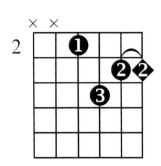

2

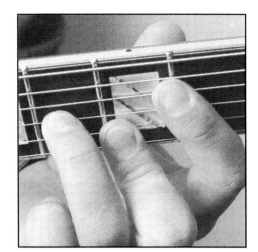

G 6

```
T  7
A  5
B  7
   5
```

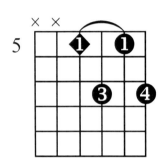

5

G 6/B

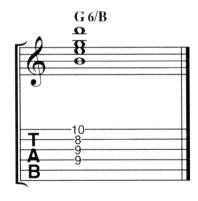

```
T  10
A  8
B  9
   9
```

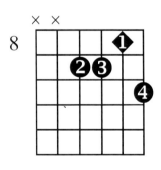

8

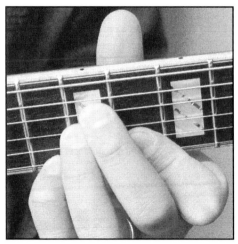

G 6/D

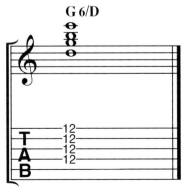

```
T  12
A  12
B  12
   12
```

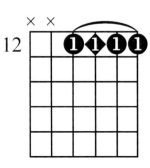

12

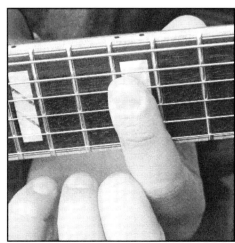

Note: the chords on this page are moveable and can be played in any of the twelve keys. See page 6 for more information.

m7 Chords

G m7/F

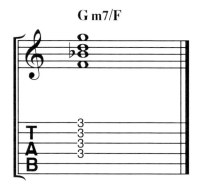
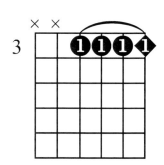
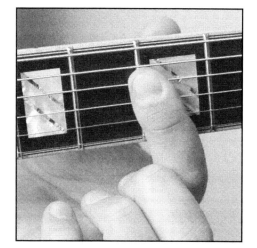

G m7

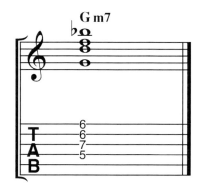
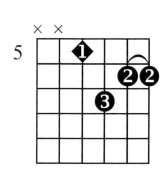
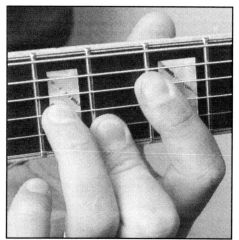

G m7/B♭

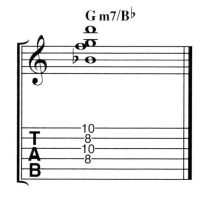
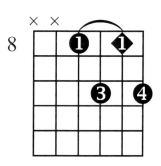

G m7/D

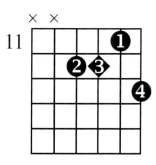

Note: the chords on this page are moveable and can be played in any of the twelve keys. See page 6 for more information.

m6 Chords

G m6/E

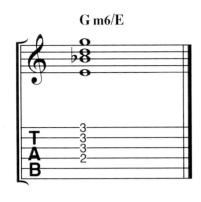

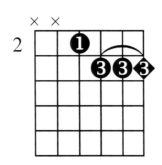

2

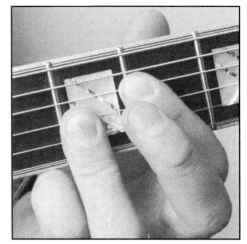

G m6

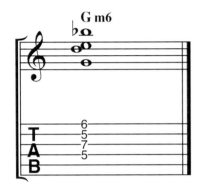

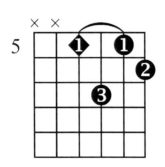

5

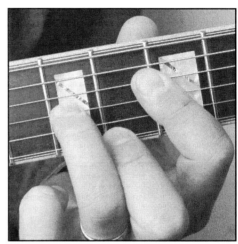

G m6/B♭

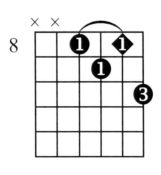

8

G m6/D

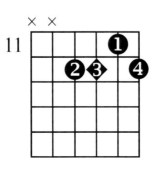

11

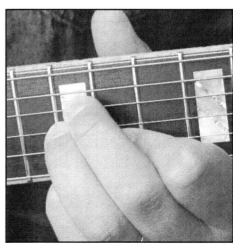

Note: the chords on this page are moveable and can be played
in any of the twelve keys. See page 6 for more information.

m7(♭5)

(º7)

G m7(♭5)/F

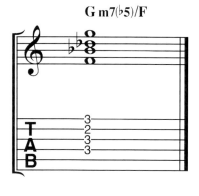

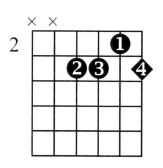

G m7(♭5)

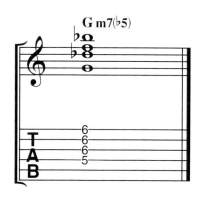

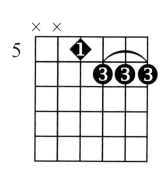

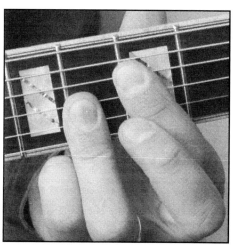

G m7(♭5)/B♭

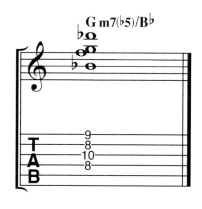

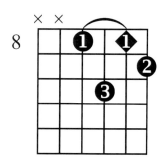

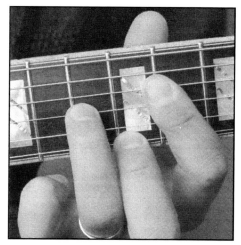

G m7(♭5)/D♭

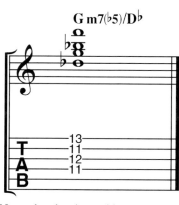

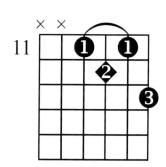

Note: the chords on this page are moveable and can be played in any of the twelve keys. See page 6 for more information.

Diminished 7th Chords

(dim7 or °7)

G dim7/E (F♭)

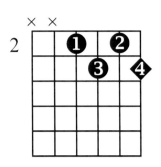

2

G dim7

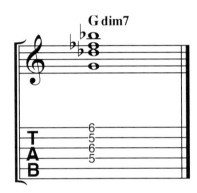

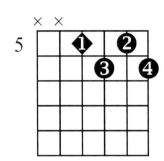

5

G dim7/B♭

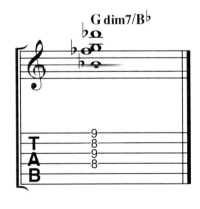

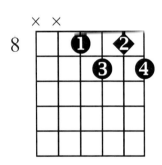

8

G dim7/D♭

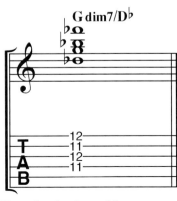

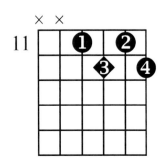

11

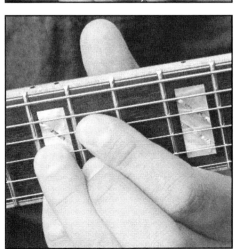

Note: the chords on this page are moveable and can be played in any of the twelve keys. See page 6 for more information.

These next shapes are commonly used with "four-to-the-bar comping." This is often referred to as "Ala Freddie Green" on many lead sheets and big band guitar music. Having only three notes, these chords are not complete seventh chords which results, at times, in similar shapes having different names. For example a G6/B, G7/B and GMaj7/B are voiced the same since the notes which separate these three chords (E, F and F♯) are not used. The chords are not full seventh or sixth chords, but represent voicings that can be used for the most common chords found in jazz charts requiring four-to-the-bar comping. These chords can prove to be invaluable when playing many jazz charts and will provide sounds that don't often clash with a full rhythm section. These voicings fit well between the register of the bass and where a piano often comps.

Also, it might be helpful to know that when playing four-to-the-bar comping, rhythm guitarists will often reduce embellished chords to basic seventh, major seventh or minor seventh chords. For example, a basic G7 can substitute for G9, G11, or G13. A GMaj7 voicing can substitute for GMaj9, GMaj13, etc. This little trick has helped many guitarists get out of sticky comping situations.

Three-Note Voicings
(Four to the Bar/ala Freddie Green Style Comping) – Maj7 Chords

G Maj7

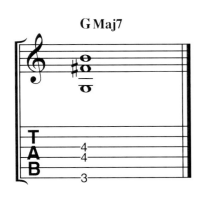

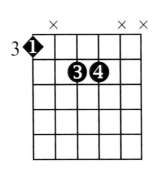

G Maj7/B

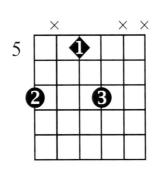

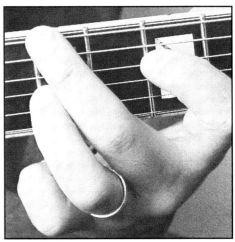

*Technically, this chord is a triad (G/B), not a Maj7 chord.
It can be used in place of a Maj7 chord.

G Maj7/D

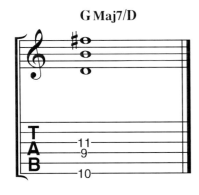

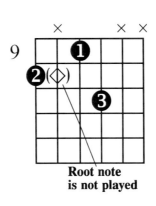

Root note
is not played

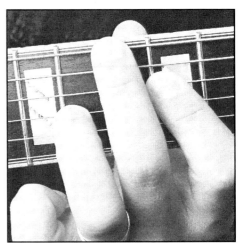

G Maj7/F#

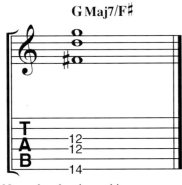

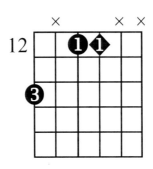

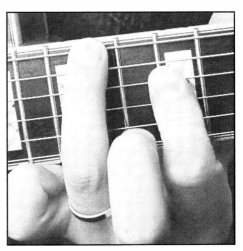

Note: the chords on this page are moveable and can be played
in any of the twelve keys. See page 6 for more information.

7th Chords

G 7

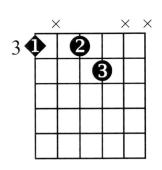

G 7/B

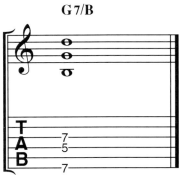

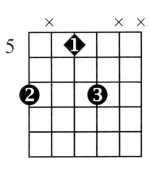

*Technically, this chord is a triad (G/B), not a 7th chord.
It can be used in place of a 7th chord.

G 7/D

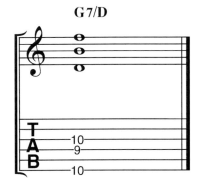

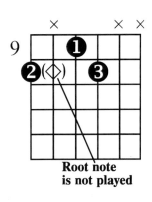

Root note
is not played

G 7/F

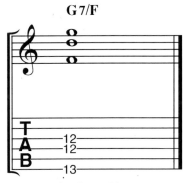

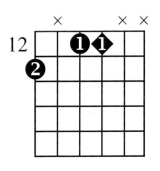

Note: the chords on this page are moveable and can be played
in any of the twelve keys. See page 6 for more information.

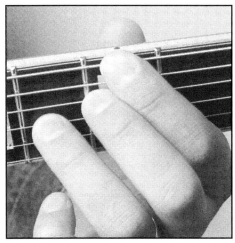

6th Chords

G 6

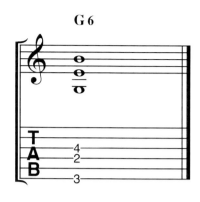

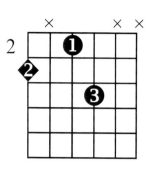

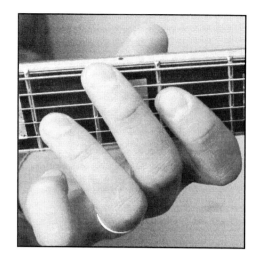

G 6/B

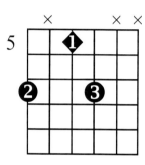

*Technically, this chord is a triad (G/B), not a 6th chord.
It can be used in place of a 6th chord.

G 6/D

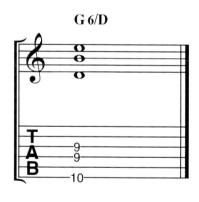

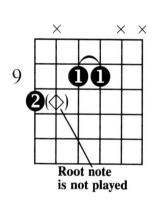

**Root note
is not played**

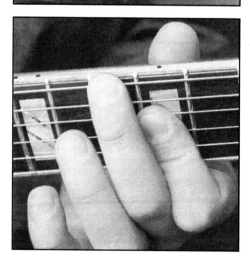

G 6/E

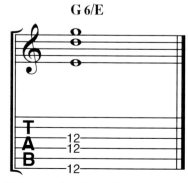

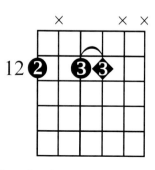

Note: the chords on this page are moveable and can be played
in any of the twelve keys. See page 6 for more information.

m7 Chords

G m7

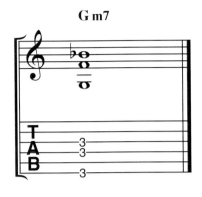

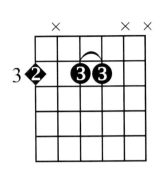

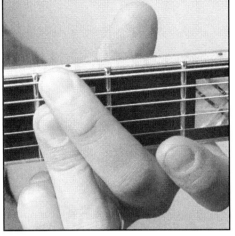

G m7/B♭

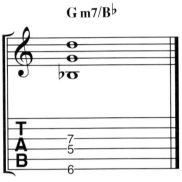

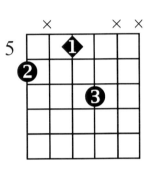

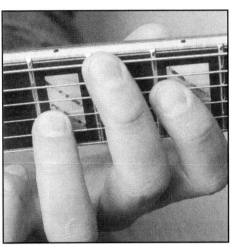

*Technically, this chord is a triad (Gm/B♭), not a m7 chord.
It can be used in place of a m7 chord.

G m7/D

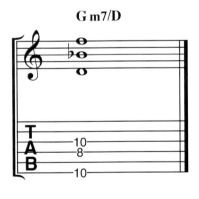

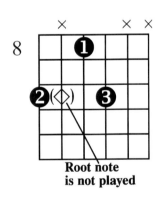

Root note
is not played

G m7/F

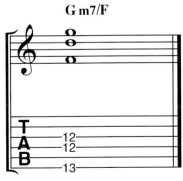

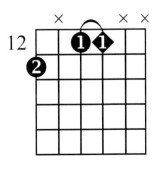

Note: the chords on this page are moveable and can be played
in any of the twelve keys. See page 6 for more information.

m6 Chords

G m6

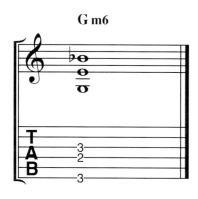
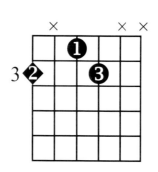
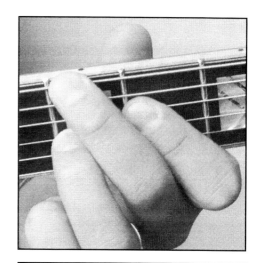

G m6/B♭

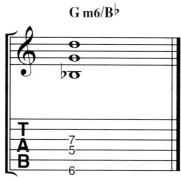
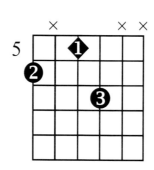

*Technically, this chord is a triad (Gm/B♭), not a m6 chord.
It can be used in place of a m6 chord.

G m6/D

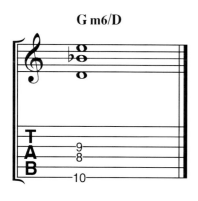
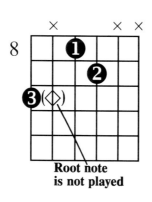

**Root note
is not played**

G m6/E

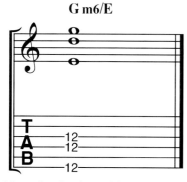
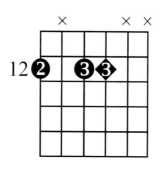

Note: the chords on this page are moveable and can be played
in any of the twelve keys. See page 6 for more information.

m7(♭5) Chords
(°7)

G m7(♭5)

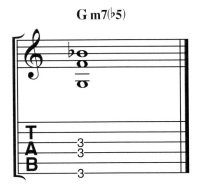
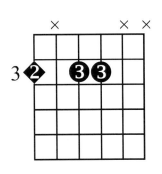
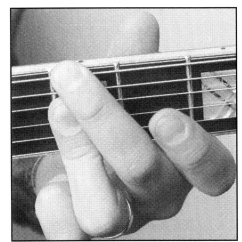

G m7(♭5)/B♭

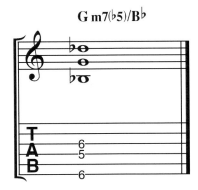
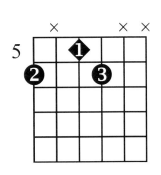

G m7(♭5)/D♭

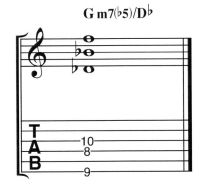
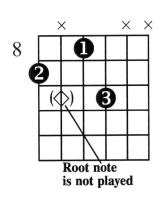

Root note
is not played

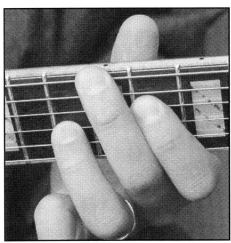

G m7(♭5)/F

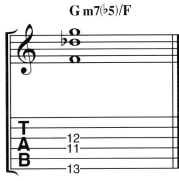
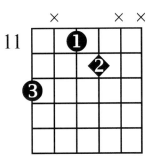

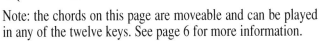

Note: the chords on this page are moveable and can be played
in any of the twelve keys. See page 6 for more information.

Diminished 7th Chords

(°7)

G dim7

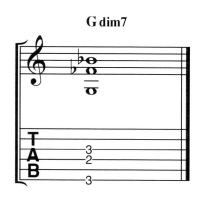
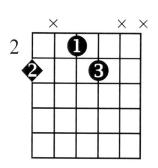
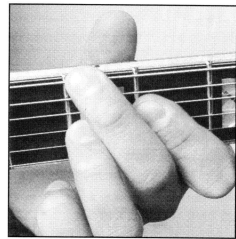

G dim7/B♭

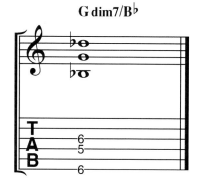
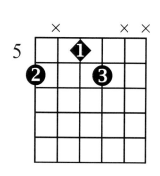
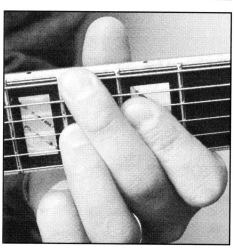

G dim7/D♭

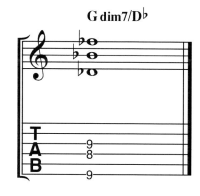
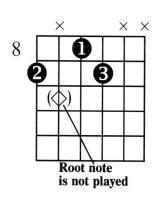

Root note
is not played

G dim7/E (F♭)

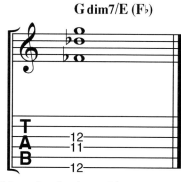
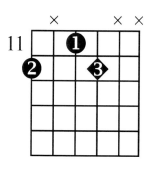
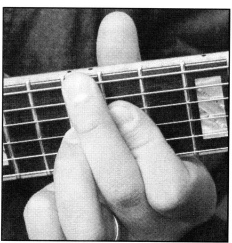

Note: the chords on this page are moveable and can be played
in any of the twelve keys. See page 6 for more information.

Here are a few other three-note voicings. These are presented with the 5th string as the lowest note, and therefore will be presented in the key of C.

Other Three-Note Voicings

C Maj7

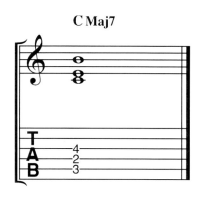
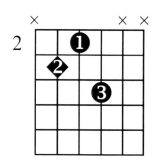

C 7

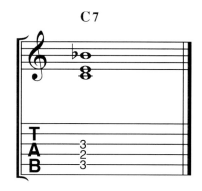
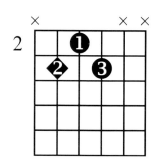
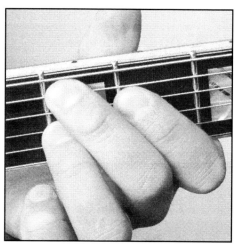

C 6

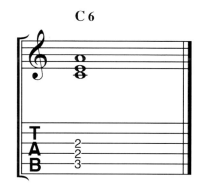
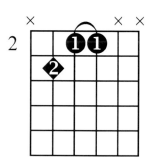

C m7

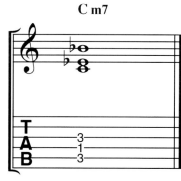
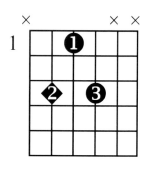

Note: the chords on this page are moveable and can be played
in any of the twelve keys. See page 6 for more information.

C m6

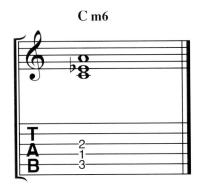

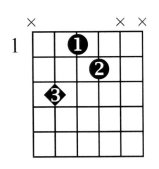

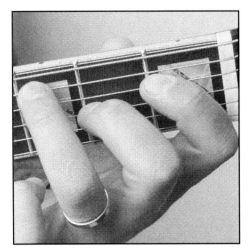

C dim7

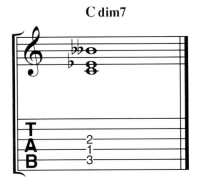

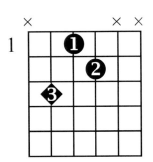

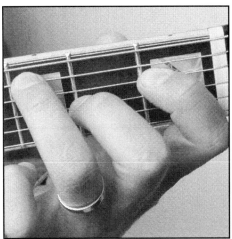

Note: the chords on this page are moveable and can be played
in any of the twelve keys. See page 6 for more information.

Here are a number of shapes and voicings for various 9th chords.

Common 9th Chords

Maj9 Chords

GMaj9

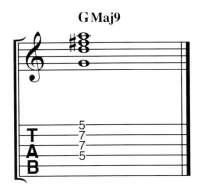

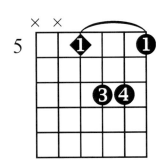

GMaj9

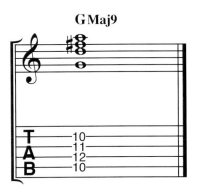

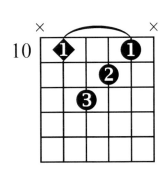

GMaj9/F#

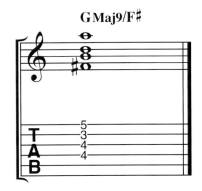

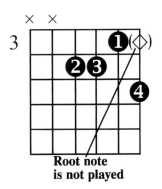

Root note
is not played

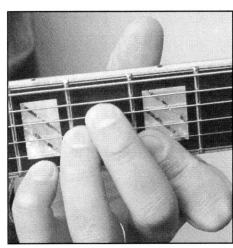

Note: the chords on this page are moveable and can be played
in any of the twelve keys. See page 6 for more information.

9th Chords

G 9

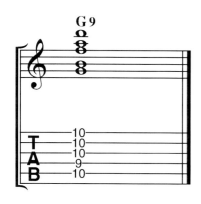

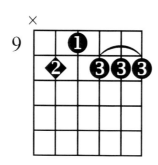

G 9/B

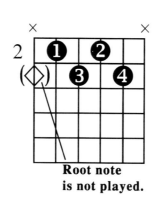

Root note
is not played.

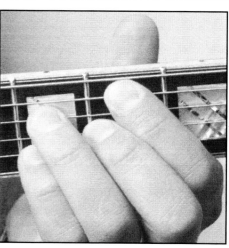

G 9/F

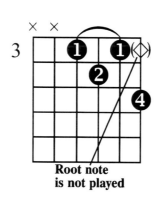

Root note
is not played

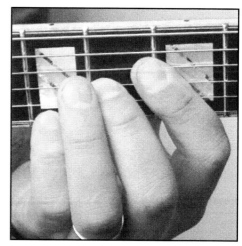

G 9/F

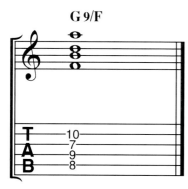

Root note
is not played

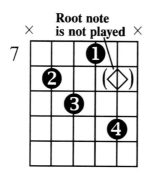

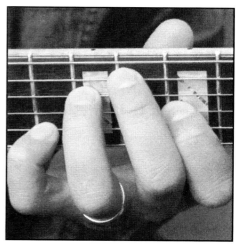

Note: the chords on this page are moveable and can be played
in any of the twelve keys. See page 6 for more information.

6/9 Chords

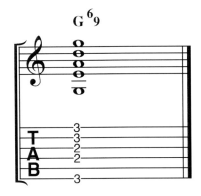

G 6 9

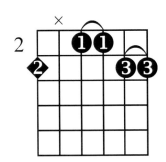

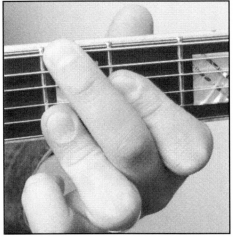

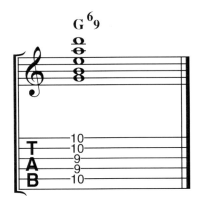

G 6 9

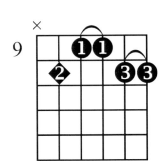

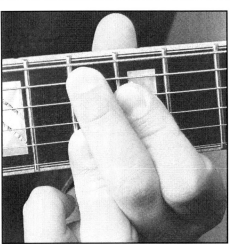

Note: the chords on this page are moveable and can be played
in any of the twelve keys. See page 6 for more information.

Common m9 Chords

G m9

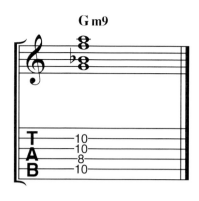

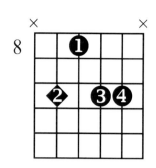

8

G m9

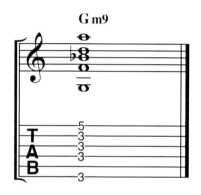

3

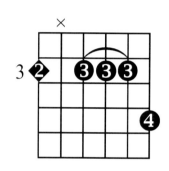

G m9/F

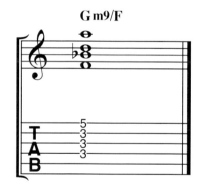

3

**Root note
is not played**

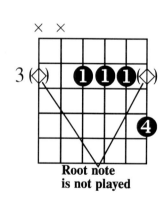

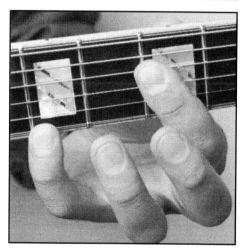

G m9/A

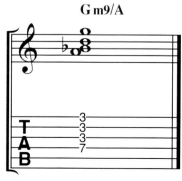

3

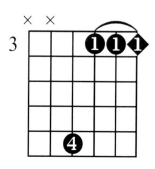

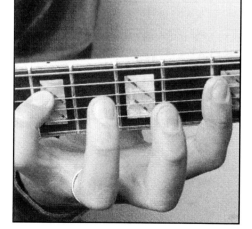

Note: the chords on this page are moveable and can be played
in any of the twelve keys. See page 6 for more information.

Many voicings for 11th chords are shown in this section.

Common 11th Chords

G11

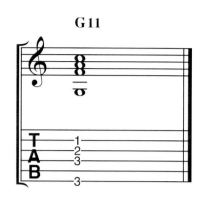
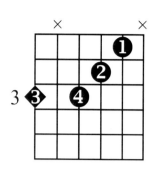
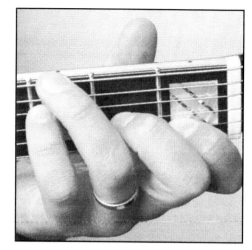

G11

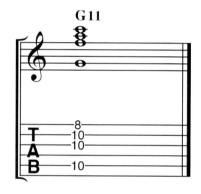
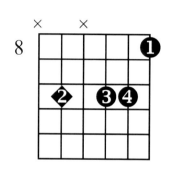
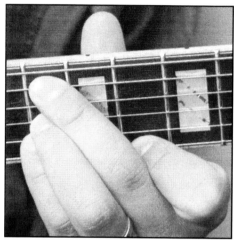

G11

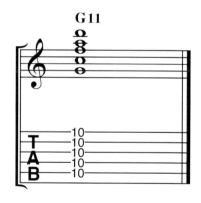
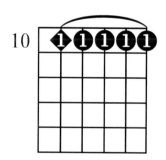
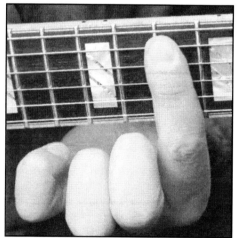

G11

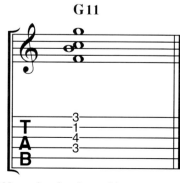
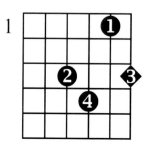
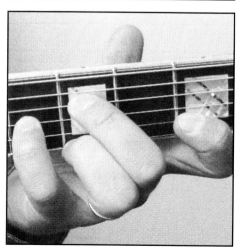

Note: the chords on this page are moveable and can be played in any of the twelve keys. See page 6 for more information.

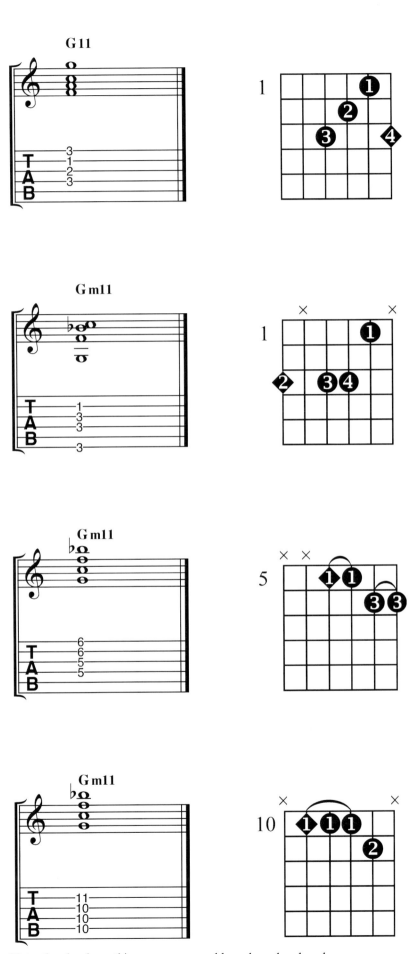

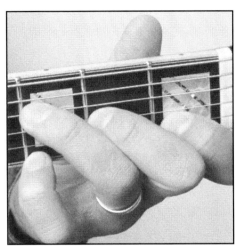

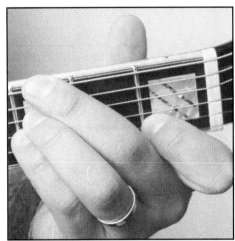

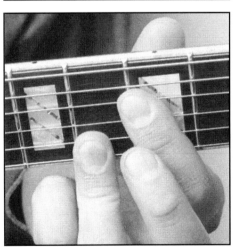

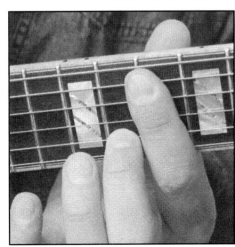

Note: the chords on this page are moveable and can be played in any of the twelve keys. See page 6 for more information.

49

Here are some 13th chords that are commonly used.

Common 13th Chords

G 13

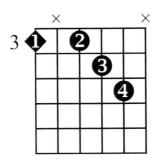

3

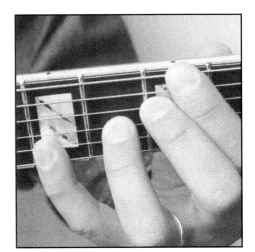

G 13

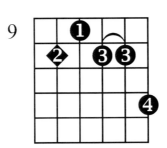

9

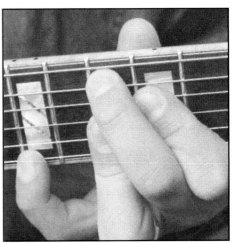

G 13

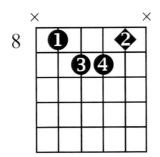

8

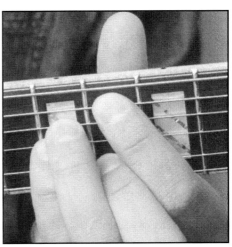

Note: the chords on this page are moveable and can be played
in any of the twelve keys. See page 6 for more information.

G 13

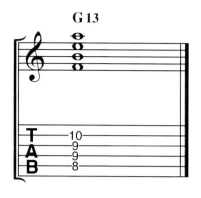

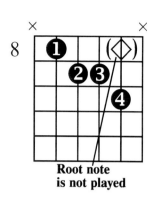

8

Root note
is not played

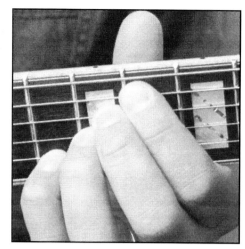

G 13

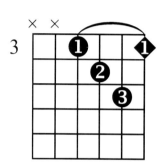

3

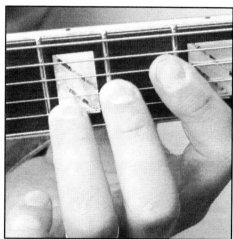

G 13

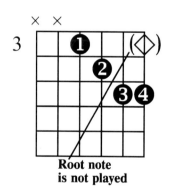

3

Root note
is not played

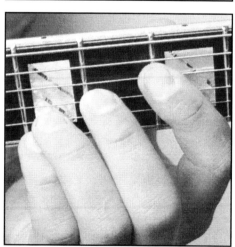

Note: the chords on this page are moveable and can be played
in any of the twelve keys. See page 6 for more information.

The following sections provide a number of other common chords that one might encounter while playing jazz standards. These include all types of major, minor and dominant seventh chords which have alterations or embellishments. These can be great sounding chords when used wisely.

Maj7(♯11) Chords

G Maj7(♯11)

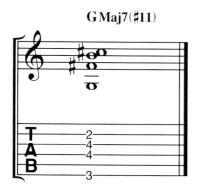

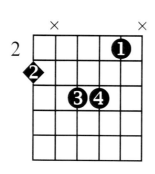

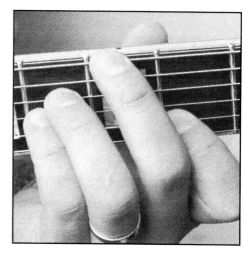

G Maj7(♯11)

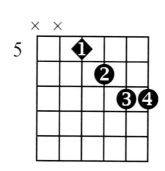

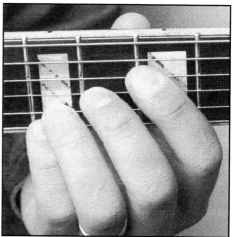

G Maj7(♯11)

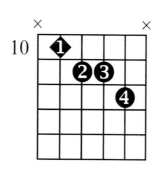

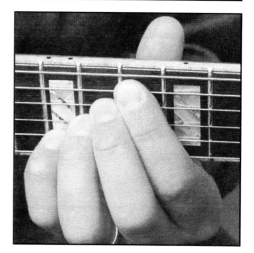

G Maj7(♯11)

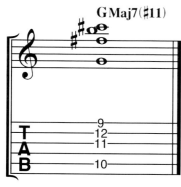

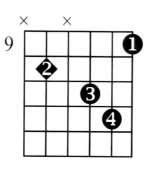

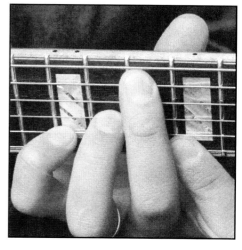

Note: the chords on this page are moveable and can be played in any of the twelve keys. See page 6 for more information.

Altered Dominant Chords
7(♭5) Chords

G 7(♭5)

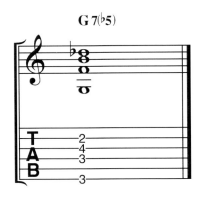

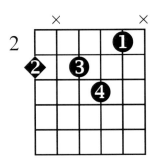

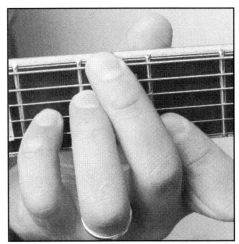

G 7(♭5)/F

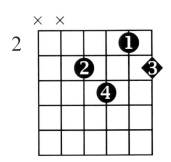

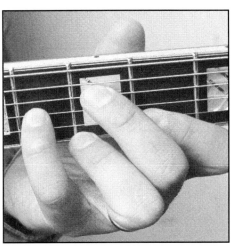

G 7(♭5)

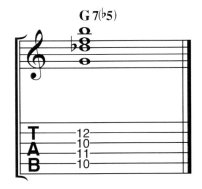

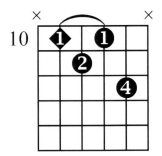

Note: the chords on this page are moveable and can be played in any of the twelve keys. See page 6 for more information.

7(♯5) Chords

G 7(♯5)

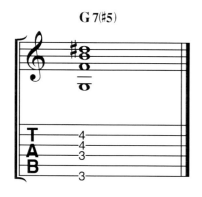 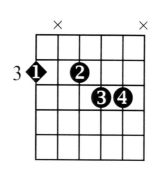 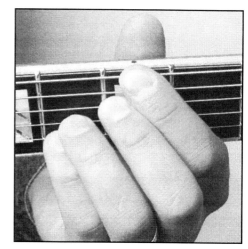

G 7(♯5)/F

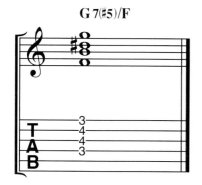 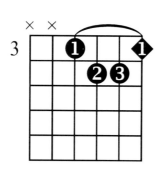 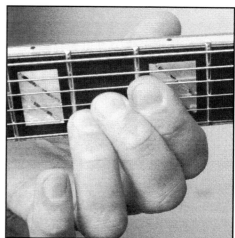

G 7(♯5)

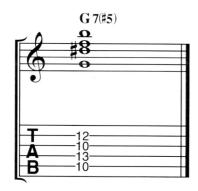 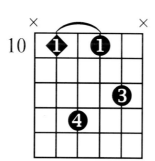 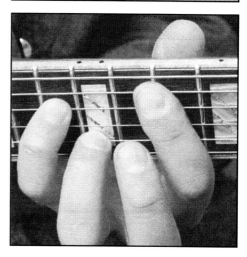

Note: the chords on this page are moveable and can be played
in any of the twelve keys. See page 6 for more information.

7(♭9) Chords

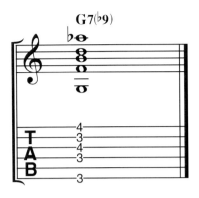

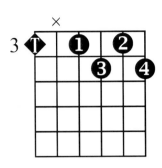

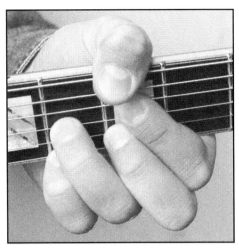

On guitar, the 7(♭9) chord is often voiced like a diminished chord. The ♭9 replaces the root. Therefore, all diminished voicings will theoretically work for the 7(♭9) chord as long as any note in the diminished chord is one fret (a half-step) above the desired root note for the 7(♭9) chord.

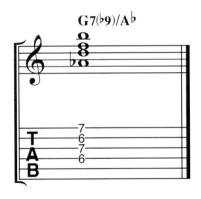

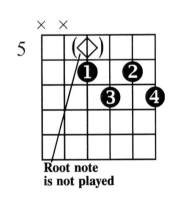

Root note is not played

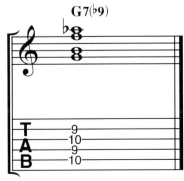

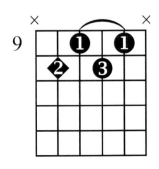

Note: the chords on this page are moveable and can be played in any of the twelve keys. See page 6 for more information.

7(♯9) Chords

G 7(♯9)

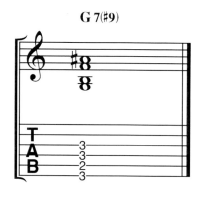 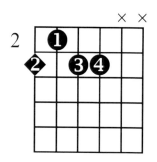 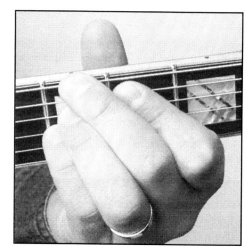

G 7(♯9)

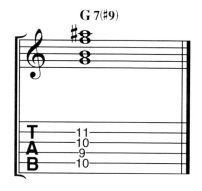 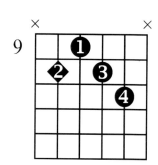 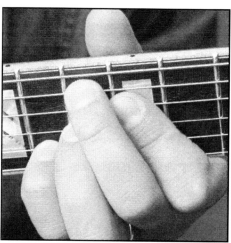

G 7(♯9)/F

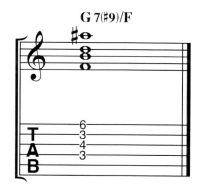 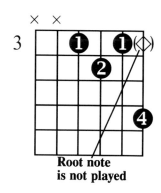

**Root note
is not played**

Note: the chords on this page are moveable and can be played
in any of the twelve keys. See page 6 for more information.

Other Altered Dominant Chords

G 7(♭5♭9)

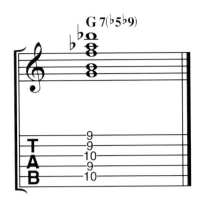
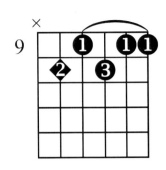

G 7(♭5♭9)/F

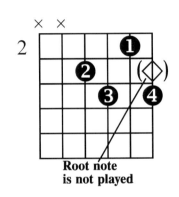

Root note
is not played

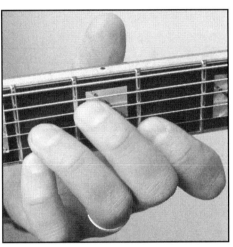

G 7(♯5♭9)

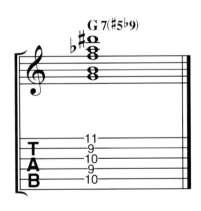
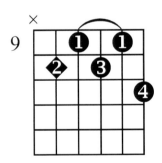
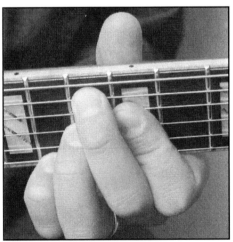

G 7(♯5♭9)

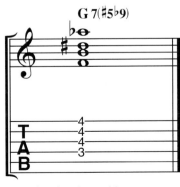

Root note
is not played

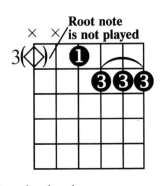
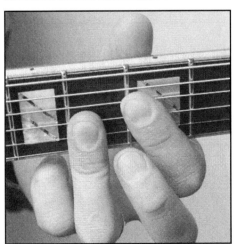

Note: the chords on this page are moveable and can be played
in any of the twelve keys. See page 6 for more information.

60

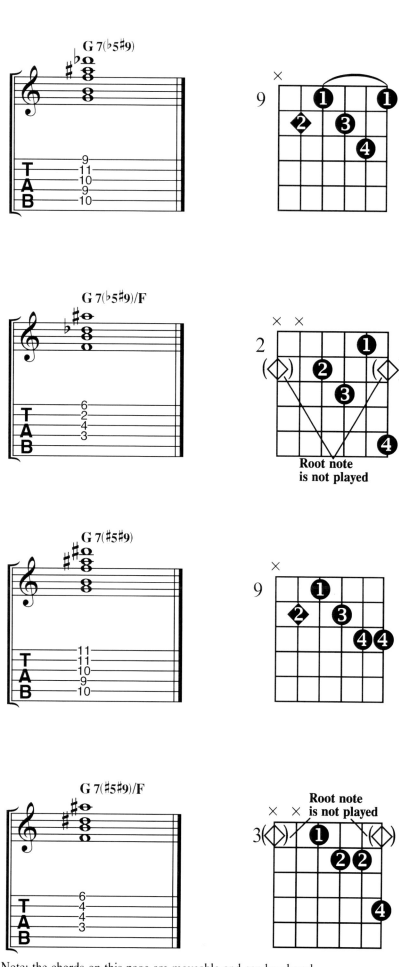

G 7(♭5♯9)

```
T
A    9
B    11
     10
     9
     10
```

G 7(♭5♯9)/F

```
T
A    6
B    2
     4
     3
```

Root note
is not played

G 7(♯5♯9)

```
T
A    11
B    11
     10
     9
     10
```

G 7(♯5♯9)/F

```
T
A    6
B    4
     4
     3
```

Root note
is not played

Note: the chords on this page are moveable and can be played
in any of the twelve keys. See page 6 for more information.

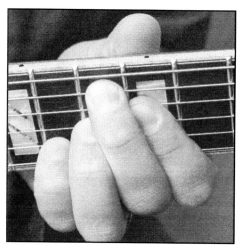

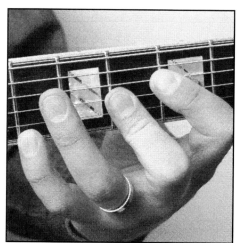

Maj7(♯5) Chords

G Maj7(♯5)

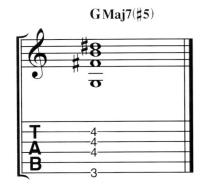 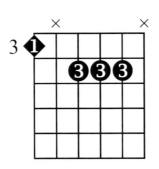 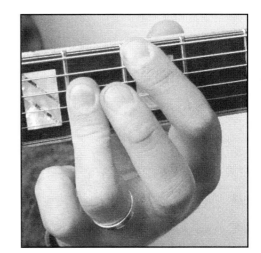

G Maj7(♯5)

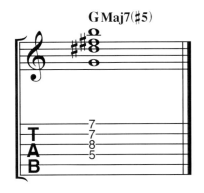 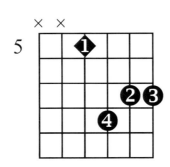 

G Maj7(♯5)

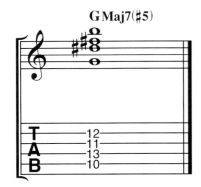 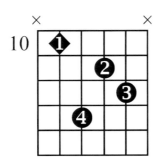 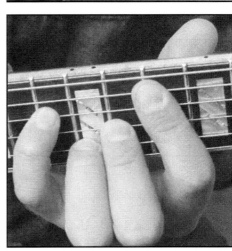

Note: the chords on this page are moveable and can be played
in any of the twelve keys. See page 6 for more information.

62

m7(♯5) Chords

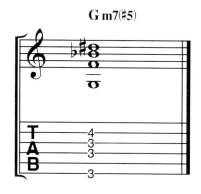
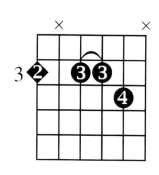

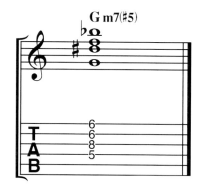
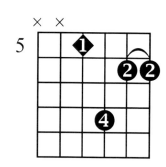
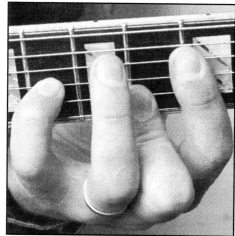

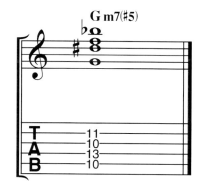
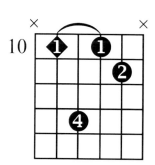
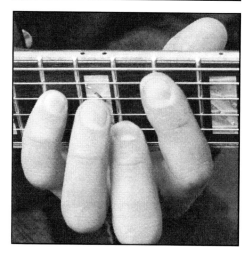

Note: the chords on this page are moveable and can be played
in any of the twelve keys. See page 6 for more information.

Scale Degrees for Commonly Used Chords

Chord Name (Chord Symbol)	Chord Tones
Major	root (note with the same letter name of the chord), 3, 5
minor	root, ♭3, 5
dim	root, ♭3, ♭5
aug	root, 3, ♯5
sus	root, 4, 5
6	root, 3, 5, 6
m6	root, ♭3, 5, 6
Maj7	root, 3, 5, 7
Maj7(♯11)	root, 3, 5, 7, ♯11[♭5]
7	root, 3, 5, ♭7
+7 [7+]	root, 3, ♯5, ♭7
7sus	root, 4, 5, ♭7
m7	root, ♭3, 5, ♭7
m7sus	root, ♭3, 4, 5, ♭7
m(Maj7)	root, ♭3, 5, 7
m7(♭5) [m7-5] [ø7]	root, ♭3, ♭5, ♭7
dim7 [°7]	root, ♭3, ♭5, ♭♭7
Maj9	root, 3, 5, 7, 9
Maj9(♯11) [Maj9+11]	root, 3, 5, 7, 9, ♯11 [♭5]
9	root, 3, 5, ♭7, 9
m9	root, ♭3, 5, ♭7, 9
add9	root, 3, 5, 9
6/9	root, 3, 5, 6, 9
6/9(♯11) [6/9+11]	root, 3, 5, 6, 9, ♯11 [♭5]
11	root, 3, 5, ♭7, 9, 11
13	root, 3, 5, ♭7, 9, 11, 13
7(♭5) [7-5]	root, 3, ♭5, ♭7
7(♯5) [7+5]	root, 3, ♯5, ♭7
7(♭9) [7-9]	root, 3, ♭5, ♭7, ♭9
7(♯9) [7+9]	root, 3, 5, ♭7, ♯9